90 Days of Prayer

A Prayer Journal for Social Workers

By
Shara Ruffin

Published by Skinny Brown Dog Media
www.SkinnyBrownDogMedia.com

ISBN 978-1-7370393-7-2

New King James Version is the source file for all Bible quotes, unless otherwise noted.

Introduction

Welcome to 90 Days of Prayer: A Prayer Journal for Social Workers Taking Their Licensing Exams. This prayer journal was inspired by my decade long journey to get my LCSW (Licensed Clinical Social Worker) license.

I experienced many hardships and life events during those ten years that could have deterred me from getting my license including having a still born daughter; failed military marriage; post-partum depression; generalized anxiety disorder; attention deficit disorder; learning disability; failing my master level licensure exam the first time. I missed the LSW exam by three points. I failed LCSW exam the first time by two points. When I took my LCSW exam the second time, I kept a prayer journal with scriptures that would give me strength during the preparation of my examination process over the course of 90 Days as a coping mechanism to help me cultivate and maintain a spiritual mindset and a relationship with GOD during the study process.

I hope that with this prayer journal, you are able to stay encouraged in your study process each day.

Shara Ruffin, LCSW, ACSW, C-SWHC, BC-TMH

A Prayer For Test Day

Dear Lord, as I take this exam, I thank you that my value is not based on my performance, but on your great love for me. Come into my heart so that we can walk through this time together. Help me not only with this test, but the many tests that life often presents. Give me the strength to endure four hours of this licensing exam. May I go in the testing room with your love, strength and encourage during the testing process.

Shara Ruffin, LCSW, ACSW, C-SWHC, BC-TMH

"Let us hold fast the profession of our faith without wavering; (for he is faithful that promised."

Hebrew 10:23

Prayer Request

Reflection

"As you read this scripture, know that you are not alone in your licensing journey. Our father is with you every step of the way. His grace is sufficient in every challenge we face on this earth and in our daily lives. He walks with us even in the darkest times. Trust in him, in his word, in his lessons that he desires to teach you on your journey."

Write your thoughts here.

Prayer Request

"May the God of hope fill you with all joy and peace as you trust in him, so that you may overflow with hope by the power of the Holy Spirit."

Roman 15:13

Reflection

"May God hold you in his bosom with hope, joy, peace as you embark each day in your licensing journey." What is hope to you and how can you cultivate hope in your licensing journey and as you work toward your exam date?

Write your thoughts here.

"Fear not, for I am with you; be not dismayed, for I am your God; I will strengthen you, I will help you, I will uphold you with my righteous right hand."

Isaiah 41:10

Prayer Request

Reflection

"Give your fear of taking the licensing exam to Christ, for he has assured promises of God. During your licensing journey and study process, how have you dealt with fear and how can you give it to God?"

Write your thoughts here.

Prayer Request

For I know the plans I have for you", declares the LORD, "Plans to proper you and not to harm you, plans to give you hope and a future."

Jeremiah 29:11

Reflection

"As Christians we face many difficulties, often our faith is tested. Your licensing journey, especially your studying process is a small part of your life, but it has an impact on your career trajectory. As you move forward daily in your process, know that God has a plan for you."

Write your thoughts here.

"Taste and see that the Lord is good; blessed is the one who takes refuge in him."

Psalm 34:8

Reflection

"Trusting in your own process through the eyes of God. Seek guidance and understanding through prayer."

Write your thoughts here.

Prayer Request

"In whom ye also trusted, after that ye heard the word of truth, the gospel of your salvation: in whom also after that ye believed, ye were sealed with that holy Spirit of promise."

Ephesians 1:13

Reflection

"Pray to our heavenly father, let him hold your troubles, your worries, your anxiety related to the licensing journey. Jesus already knows what is in your heart to bear. Bear it in this space, pray and leave it to him."

Write your thoughts here.

Prayer Request

"Casting all your anxieties on him, because he cares for you."

1 Peter 5:7

Reflection

"Jesus already knows your struggles in your licensing journey. When we cast all our worries to God, he will give you the peace that passes all understanding."

Write your thoughts here.

_____

_____

_____

_____

_____

_____

_____

_____

Prayer Request

> "For I am convinced that neither death nor life, neither angels nor demons, neither the present nor the future, nor any powers, neither height nor depth, nor anything else in all creation, will be able to separate us from the love of God that is in Christ Jesus our Lord."

Roman 8:38-39

Reflection

"When we hear the encouraging words of God, we must surrender our faith to him. Know that hard things will happen during your journey through your licensing process, but do not surrender to those hard times, get down on your knees and pray. Our Heavenly Father will hold our burdens as we move forward in our purpose."

Write your thoughts here.

Prayer Request

"The steadfast love of the LORD never ceases; his mercies never come to an end: they are new every morning; great is your faithfulness."

Lamentations 3:22-23

Reflection

"The Love of God is forever, even in our darkest hour, know that your journey is not in vain, your gifts are being cultivated as you move through your study process. God will wrap you in his arms and hold you, when you can not hold yourself, even during times of struggle. Hold on, put the work in and let GOD, hold the rest."

Write your thoughts here.

Prayer Request

"So we do not lose heart. Through our outer self is wasting away, our inner self is being renewed day by day. For this light momentary affliction is preparing for us an eternal weight of glory beyond all comparison, as well look not to the things that are seen but to the things that are unseen."

2: Corinthians 4:16-18

Reflection

"Our struggles are not for us, it becomes the blueprint for others, know that during your study process, with each day that you put the work into your process, it is the work of GOD and even when you can't see the rest of your journey, know that each day that you open your study materials, God is there, he is listening to your prayers and the matters of your heart."

Write your thoughts here.

Prayer Request

"The LORD is my light and my salvation: whom shall I fear? The LORD is the stronghold of my life; of whom shall I be afraid?"

Psalm 27:1

Reflection

"When you are carving your journey, know that GOD has already done it for you, each day that you open your study materials, trust in your process, trust in GOD, that he will carry you through the inner storms of doubts, fears, anxiety. We have nothing to fear if we trust in him."

Write your thoughts here.

"Therefore do not worry about tomorrow, for tomorrow will worry about itself. Each day has enough trouble of its own."

Matthews 6:34

Reflection

"Focus on the present and each day in front of you. For all we have is the present. It is unique gift of life, those precious moments that we see the wonders of GOD and his glory. Let us take comfort in our heavenly Father that he allows us to live moment to moment. Take each day of your study process as a gift to be better and to cultivate the knowledge needed to be prepared for your exam."

Write your thoughts here.

Prayer Request

"There is no fear in love. But perfect love drives out fear, because fear has to do with punishment. The one who fears is not made perfect in love."

John 4:18

Reflection

"John 4:18 speaks of love. Love is patient and kind. May we never forget that love is not perfect, it is not selfish, immature nor childish. Love bears all things and endures through all things. During your licensing journey, whether that is gaining clinical hours toward your advanced license or preparing for licensing exam. Know that God loves you, fear not what lays before you. Fall into that love through prayer to our heavenly father."

Write your thoughts here.

"I wait for the **LORD**, my whole being waits, and his word I put my hope."

Psalm 130:5

Reflection

"Trust in GOD that he will lead you through the journey, for he already knows the matters of your heart. Let him fill you with hope and peace. Cultivating joy in your process of gaining knowledge to serve others."

Write your thoughts here.

_____

_____

_____

_____

_____

_____

_____

_____

_____

Prayer Request

> "Be strong and let your heart take courage, all you who wait for the LORD."

Psalm 31:24

Reflection

"The journey may be long, but it is worth it. All your long days of studying, balancing the demands of life will pay off in time. Pray for guidance, Pray for strength, Pray for Mercy. In the eyes of GOD all things are possible."

Write your thoughts here.

....

....

....

....

....

....

....

....

....

Prayer Request

> "If any of you lack wisdom, let him ask of God, that giveth to all men liberally, and upbraideth not; and it shall be given him."

James 1:5

Reflection

"The Lord will never abandon you, you may feel at times you are alone in your path toward your license, but there were many before you that have walked this path and there will be many after you that will walk this path. Trust GOD. Pray to him to give you what you need to keep going forward, despite your fears and doubts. For the Lord knows them and will keep you, if you stick to your process."

Write your thoughts here.

"But they who wait for the LORD shall renew their strength; they shall mount up with wings like eagles; they shall run and not be weary; they shall walk and not faint."

Isaiah 40:31

Prayer Request

Reflection

"When you put your trust in God and allow him to lead your life, your path will unfold naturally. As you work through your licensing journey, know that the path will not be easy, but the lessons you learn along the way through GOD's grace will be what pulls you forward. God's understanding is unsearchable. When you wait upon the LORD, your prayers will be answered. In Jesus name Amen."

Write your thoughts here.

"For I reckon that the sufferings of this present time are not worthy to be compared with the glory which shall be revealed in us."

Roman 8:18

Prayer Request

Reflection

"With God it is possible, believe in him throughout your journey, for he will make a way out of no way. At times it will be difficult to study, when daily life can pull you from focus, but get down on knees and pray GOD for grace and clarity to help you get on track with your process. We all lose focus, but it is our job to put faith in our GOD and in your ability to focus and prepare for your exams. GET THE PASS!"

Write your thoughts here.

_____

_____

_____

_____

_____

_____

_____

_____

_____

Prayer Request

"I can do all things through him who strengthens me."

Philippians 4:13

Reflection

"When we give our worries to GOD, he makes a way for us. Trust in him to give you strength, focus, consistency to work each day toward your goal of achieving licensure, no matter what part of your process that you are in. Through our heavenly father, we can endure all things with his love and strength. Choose to endure and GOD will give you strength and focus to achieve."

Write your thoughts here.

Prayer Request

"Therefore my beloved brothers, be steadfast immovable, always abounding in the work of the LORD, knowing that in the LORD your labor is not in vain."

1 Corinthians 15:58

Reflection

"Walking with GOD in your licensing your journey will test your faith at times, however knowing that your labor for the LORD is not in vain. Your work as a social service provider is GOD's work. Know that taking this path can be difficult and wearisome, however it is never without meaning or value in the eyes of GOD."

Write your thoughts here.

Prayer Request

"Trust in the
LORD with
all your heart,
and do not lean
on your own
understanding.
In all your ways
acknowledge him,
and he will make
straight your
paths."

Proverbs 3:3-6

Reflection

"To acknowledge God in all our ways means we should learn in everything we do in this life to line up how we do things with GOD and his ways. So, have GOD make straight paths for your feet in whatever you do, take time to learn who you are in Christ."

Write your thoughts here.

Prayer Request

"Be watchful stand firm in the faith, act like men, be strong. Let all that you do be done in love."

1 Corinthians 16:13-14

Reflection

"God has called and chosen you for this heavenly purpose. In order to achieve, you need to overcome any trials and difficult situations in this life. This goes for the licensing journey as well. Hardships and difficulties can show in different forms and its individualized to your journey as you walk through your daily path to the license. There will be others who may not understand your journey, but GOD understands. Do not let others corrupt or divide you from GOD. Fight for your Faith. Fight for your license. GET THE PASS. In Jesus name Amen."

Write your thoughts here.

Prayer Request

"Our faith can move mountains"

Matthews 17:20

Reflection

"Faith lays hold of God to do the impossible. You must have faith in what you can't see. See yourself passing this exam. Hold on to the vision that God has for you."

Write your thoughts here.

"Give thanks to the LORD for He is good; His. Love endures forever"

Psalm 107:1

Reflection

"When we give thanks to GOD for our life and for the path before us. We cultivate gratitude and in doing so we create a focus on the present and on every step we take with GOD to help us along our journey. Give thanks for each day that you are able to wake up and focus on your studies to pass the exam, because there are those that don't even make it that far. Praise him. Amen."

Write your thoughts here.

Prayer Request

"And we know that in all things God works for the good of those who love him, who have been called according to his purpose."

Romans 8:28

Reflection

"Romans 8:28 teaches us that no matter the circumstance those who love God are called according to His Purpose. During your licensing journey, know that you are walking in the purpose that GOD has set for you to walk. It is already written, you just have to put the work in and implement his will."

Write your thoughts here.

Prayer Request

"For by grace you have been saved through faith. And this is not your own doing; it is a gift of God, not a result of works, so that no one may boast."

Ephesians 2:8-9

Reflection

"We are saved by grace through faith in our Lord, not by our own efforts or works, but through GOD's love for us. Trust in that love, that God will provide what you need to pass your exam. Believe in yourself and the work of GOD."

Write your thoughts here.

Prayer Request

"For we walk by faith, not by sight."

2 Corinthians 5:7

Reflection

"During the licensing journey, sometimes we cast our doubts, fears inward and they manifest in preparation for the licensing exam, whether by second guessing ourselves and our abilities to pass the exam or simply in our anxiety. Know that GOD is with you in this process and he will guide you every step of the way, but you must have faith and you must put the work in."

Write your thoughts here.

"And Jesus answered them 'Truly, I say to you, if you have faith and do not doubt, you will not only do what has been done to the fig tree, but even if you say to this mountain, 'Be taken up and thrown into the sea,' it will happen. And whatever you ask in prayer you will receive, if you have faith."

Matthew 21:21-22

Prayer Request

Reflection

"Have faith in yourself to pass your exam. If you cannot see your vision, you will not be able to achieve the vision. Have faith in GOD and his vision for you. Walk in Faith and take each step with GOD."

Write your thoughts here.

Prayer Request

"May you strengthened with all power, according to his glorious might, for all endurance and patience with joy."

Colossians 1:11

Reflection

"God will provide you with guidance, strength and endurance during your exam process. Every day, every minute, every second of your licensing journey was meant for you. Embrace your journey and give it to God."

Write your thoughts here.

Prayer Request

"You have turned my mourning into dancing; you have loosed my sackcloth and clothed me with gladness."

Psalm 30:11

Reflection

"God provides for all that follow him. In your licensing journey you will be tested in ways you may not expect, let the LORD take your fears, apprehension, anxiety and turn them into prosperity. Open your heart and mind to your process and walk in faith with the LORD."

Write your thoughts here.

Prayer Request

"*Splendor and majesty are before him; strength and joy are in his place.*"

1 Chronicles 16:27

Reflection

"When you turn to the Lord and come before him, you will find the strength you need to beat the odds. You will find joy, hope and peace within him, that you will not find anywhere on Earth. During your licensing journey, lay before GOD your burdens and seek guidance while preparing for your licensing exam."

Write your thoughts here.

Prayer Request

> "Peace I leave with you; my peace I give you. I do not give to you as the world gives. Do not let your hearts be troubled and do not be afraid."
>
> John 14:27

Reflection

"God does not want us to fear because he already has won the victory. While you may be anxious about your path in your licensing journey, trust in that journey through God."

Write your thoughts here.

Prayer Request

> "Rejoice in hope, be patient in tribulation, be constant in prayer."
>
> Roman 12:12

Reflection

"Cultivate strength through our Lord. He is a powerful force that can hold our burdens when we cannot."

Write your thoughts here.

_____

_____

_____

_____

_____

_____

_____

_____

_____

Prayer Request

> "Rejoice in hope, be patient in tribulation, be constant in prayer."
>
> Romans 12:12

Reflection

"Be consistent in your faith and prayer throughout your licensing progress, for you are not walking alone, you are walking with GOD. Pray every step of the way from the study process to the examination room."

Write your thoughts here.

_____

_____

_____

_____

_____

_____

_____

_____

Prayer Request

"There hath no temptation taken you but such as is common to man: but God is faithful, who will not suffer you to be tempted above that ye are able; but will with the temptation also make a way to escape, that ye may be able to bear it."

1 Corinthians 10:13

Reflection

"The words of the LORD, may you take them into your study process with comfort. You were created in his image. You are not to fear. Our sins are eternally separated from the Lord, He redeemed us with the precious blood of Jesus Christ. We have been brought with a price and the required redemption price for our souls was the life of Christ, and the price has been paid in FULL. Have faith in our LORD, he knows the burdens that you bear in your licensing journey."

Write your thoughts here.

Prayer Request

> "I sought the LORD, and he answered me; he delivered me from all my fears."
>
> Psalm 34:4

Reflection

"During your licensing journey, walk with GOD, let his words delivery you from your fears of your examination. Plan prayer each day during your study process. God will hear them. He will dissipate all those fears. Give God your fears and continue each day to move forward in faith."

Write your thoughts here.

Prayer Request

"When anxiety was great within me, your consolation brought me joy"

Psalm 94:19

Reflection

"Even in the midst of adversity and anxiety, God provides encouragement and support. You were born for this journey. All your hard work to even qualify for the exam was apart of God's plan. Believe in him. Believe in your journey. Believe in your process."

Write your thoughts here.

Prayer Request

"But the fruit of the Spirit is love, joy, peace, patience, kindness, goodness, faithfulness."

Galatians 5:22

Reflection

"Living in the fruit of the spirit simply means you are in the influence of the holy spirit. You are a child of GOD. You walk with him and you will cultivate the fruits of the spirit in your study process. Believe in the stairs that you cannot see laid before you by the LORD. Take a step each day, turn a page of your study material each day and you will complete the staircase created by GOD made just for you."

Write your thoughts here.

Prayer Request

"Until now you have asked nothing in my name. Ask, and you will receive, that your joy may be full."

John 16:24

Reflection

"Without asking for what you want you will not receive. Ask for GOD to lead you in your journey and watch what happens in your study process."

Write your thoughts here.

_____

_____

_____

_____

_____

_____

_____

_____

_____

_____

Prayer Request

"A joyful heart is good medicine, but a crushed spirit dries up the bones."

Proverbs 17:22

Reflection

"Be joyful with God during your study process. Find your peace through God in your licensing journey through the bible; listen to worship music; cultivate through prayer. God invented joy for you to experience. Remember you are getting your license and fighting for your license in your study process...not necessarily for you, but for the people you haven't even reached yet. They are waiting for you to PASS amen. God is waiting to present them to you. Amen."

Write your thoughts here.

"*Whom having not seen, ye love; in whom, though now ye see him no, yet believing, ye rejoice with joy unspeakable and full of glory.*"

1 Peter 1:18

Prayer Request

Reflection

"Joy is through the love of Christ. When we follow his path, we bring forth abundance in him. Trust his love for you will plant the seeds needed to get through your licensing journey."

Write your thoughts here.

Prayer Request

"And ye now therefore have sorrow: but I will see you again, and your heart shall rejoice, and your joy no man taketh from you."

John 16:22

Reflection

"Rejoice with the Lord for he will show you the way during your licensing process, allow him. Allow yourself to walk with him in faith."

Write your thoughts here.

"This is the day that the Lord has made; let us rejoice and be glad in it."

Psalm 118:24

Prayer Request

Reflection

"Obey and rejoice with GOD in your licensing journey as you go through the motions each day. Whether you are applying for your initial license through your state boards or if your actively in your study process, know that GOD would not leave you astray. Rejoice in him and stay grounded within your licensing journey."

Write your thoughts here.

Prayer Request

"Thou wilt shew me the path of life: in thy presence is fulness of joy; at thy right hand there are pleasures for evermore."

Psalm 16:11

Reflection

"When we walk in faith, we walk with GOD and all the pleasures he can bestow upon us. Cultivate gratitude each day that you are able to study for your exam, for there are those that are not able to do so and have not qualified to do so. God has chosen you for this journey and it is your obligation to complete it."

Write your thoughts here.

Prayer Request

"These things have I spoken unto you, that my joy might remain in you, and that your joy might be full."

John 15:11

Reflection

"During your licensing journey you will face many barriers. Know that abiding in Christ is often displayed as a service of suffering. But the glorious truth is that those who patiently endure the deepest pain for righteousness sake are often those that experience the greatest joy in the Lord. Abiding in Christ and sharing in his suffering produces much good fruit - and is the means to lift us high above the storms of life. The man or woman whose life is a service of suffering is the one that has been prepared to die to self and live to Christ - presenting their body as a living sacrifice, holy and acceptable unto the Lord."

Write your thoughts here.

Prayer Request

"Therefore my heart is glad, and my glory rejoiceth: my flesh also shall rest in hope."

Psalm 16:9

Reflection

"God makes a path in life that is unique to each life that he touches. If we follow him, safety and refuge follows. With our faith in him, we cultivate security. Take comfort in your licensing journey, that as long as you call upon God in your journey to lead you by your faith, he will help you each day to take another step forward."

Write your thoughts here.

Prayer Request

"Rejoice evermore. Pray without ceasing. In everything give thanks; for this is the will of God in Christ Jesus concerning you."

1 Thessalonians 5:16-18

Reflection

"There are many ways to cultivate the peace of God in the journey to obtaining your license. These steps include obedience, praying, gratitude and most of all trusting in GOD. When we trust the Lord, we lay the foundation to the road of abundance. Know that your path was meant for you and the. License is already yours. God just needs you to claim it but first, he must test your will to seek it through examination."

Write your thoughts here.

Prayer Request

> "When the Spirit of truth comes, he will guide you into all the truth, for he will not speak on his own authority, but whatever he hears he will speak, and he will declare to you the things that are to come."
>
> John 16:13

Reflection

"There are many ways to cultivate the peace of God in the journey to obtaining your license. These steps include obedience, praying, gratitude and most of all trusting in GOD. When we trust the Lord, we lay the foundation to the road of abundance. Know that your path was meant for you and the. License is already yours. God just needs you to claim it but first, he must test your will to seek it through examination."

Write your thoughts here.

Reflectional Prayers

A Prayer To Cultivate Peace

Loving God, please grant me peace of mind and calm my troubled heart. My soul is like a turbulent sea. I can't seem to find my balance so I stumble and worry constantly. Give me the strength and clarity of mind to find my purpose and walk the path you've laid out for me. I trust your Love God, and know that you will heal this stress. Just as the sun rises each day against the dark of night. Please bring me clarity with the light of God.

Amen